25 —

12/05

What on Earth? Hurricanes

What on Earth?

Can a hurricane do any good?

Turn this page for the answer.

Published in 2005 in the United States by Children's Press,
an imprint of Scholastic Library Publishing,
90 Sherman Turnpike, Danbury, CT 06816

ISBN 0-516-25320-4 (Lib. Bdg)

A CIP catalogue record for this title is
available now from the Library of Congress.

Printed and bound in China.

Editors:	Ronald Coleman
	Sophie Izod
Senior Art Editor:	Carolyn Franklin
DTP Designer:	Mark Williams

Picture Credits Julian Baker & Janet Baker (J B
Illustrations): 6-7, 8, 9(t), Nick Hewetson: 3, 10-11, 18, 20-
21, Corbis: 1, 13, 16, 17, 24-25, 28, Digital Vision: 14-15,
19, 23, 26, 29, Douglas R. Clifford/St. Petersburg
Times/Florida: 9(b), NASA Langley Research Center: 30-31,
NASDA/NASA/JPL: 15

Cover © Douglas R. Clifford/St. Petersburg Times/Florida

What on Earth?

Yes!

Hurricanes cause water
surges which spread coral
eggs and help more coral
to grow.

What on Earth?

Hurricanes

CATHERINE CHAMBERS

What do satellites have to do with hurricanes?

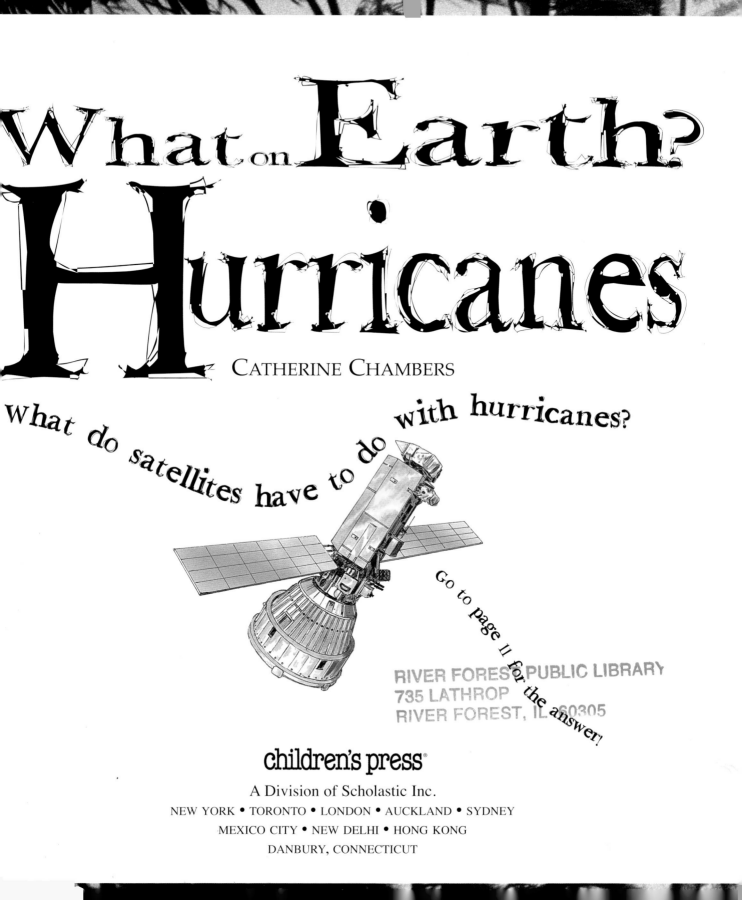

Go to page 11 for the answer!

RIVER FOREST PUBLIC LIBRARY
735 LATHROP
RIVER FOREST, IL 60305

children's press®

A Division of Scholastic Inc.

NEW YORK • TORONTO • LONDON • AUCKLAND • SYDNEY
MEXICO CITY • NEW DELHI • HONG KONG
DANBURY, CONNECTICUT

Contents

What on Earth?

Hurricane Floyd

In 1999 Hurricane Floyd brought so much rain to the United States that thirteen states declared themselves disaster zones.

Introduction

A hurricane is a violent tropical storm that forms over an ocean. It is a whirling spiral of wind that thunders across Earth's surface at speeds of more than 74 miles (119 kilometers) per hour.

How strong is a hurricane?

A hurricane is no ordinary storm. Its winds can uproot massive trees, blow down bridges and easily rip the roofs from buildings. It brings with it driving rain and crashing thunderstorms. Its effect on the ocean can also bring great danger from the sea itself.

What's inside a hurricane?

The area at the center of a hurricane is known as the "eye" of the storm. It is surrounded by a whirling spiral of wind. When the "eye" is overhead, the hurricane conditions come to a stop. The sky becomes blue again and for a short time, all is calm.

What Is a Hurricane?

The effects of a hurricane are felt in three separate stages. The first phase of a hurricane is vicious – with raging winds, torrents of rain and fierce thunder and lightning. As the eye of the storm passes overhead, the sun shines and all seems calm again. But then the backlash of the storm sweeps in for its second wave of destruction.

Huge circle of clouds around hurricane

Eye of the storm

Upward spiral of wind

Water vapor (water in the form of gas) in the rising air condenses to form thick clouds

Cool air billows out from the top
of the storm and forms a huge
circle of cloud

Warm, damp
air rises from
the sea

Coastline

The spinning
motion of Earth
makes the
winds travel
upwards

Winds of cool
air blow in

Rain falls
below

7

Where Do Hurricanes Happen?

Hurricanes only form over hot tropical oceans, which are on either side of the equator. They **spin** furiously towards land mostly affecting the Caribbean Islands, Central America and the east coast of the United States.

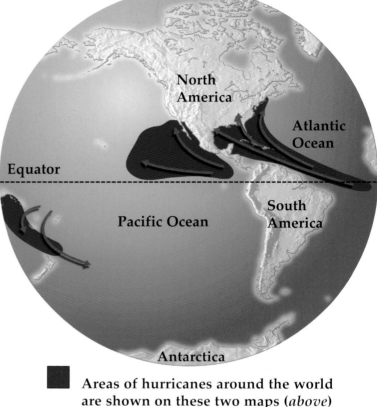

North America

Atlantic Ocean

Equator

Pacific Ocean

South America

Antarctica

Areas of hurricanes around the world are shown on these two maps (*above*)

What a lot of wind!

In the northern hemisphere cyclones spin in a counter-clockwise direction and anticyclones spin in a clockwise direction. In the southern hemisphere it's the opposite.

Polar trade winds

Cyclone

Westerlies

Anticyclone

Northeast trade winds

What is a typhoon?

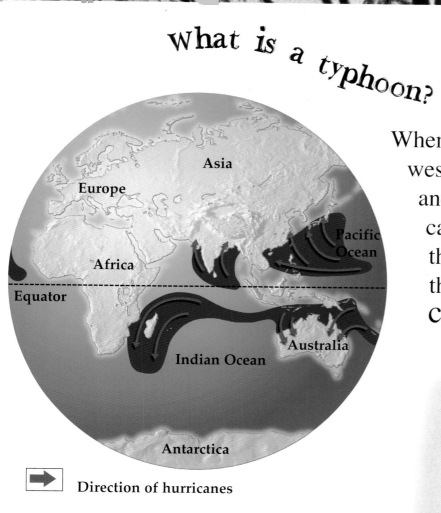

Asia

Europe

Pacific Ocean

Africa

Equator

Indian Ocean

Australia

Antarctica

➡️ Direction of hurricanes

When hurricanes happen in the western Pacific and hit Japan and the Philippines, they're called **"typhoons"**. When they hit India and Australia they are called "tropical **cyclones**".

What are hurricane force winds?

Hurricane force winds are winds that blow at the same speed as hurricanes but do not develop into full hurricanes.

Hurricane Francis hitting the east coast of Florida

Can Hurricanes Be Spotted?

Scientists can track the movement of hurricanes by watching satellite pictures. Satellite tracking has made it possible to issue **warnings** of a hurricane's likely path and ferocity. Aircraft fly into the eye of the storm to gather information about wind-speed, temperature and humidity levels inside a hurricane. The *Doppler* radar system plots the shape and speed of a hurricane.

Information is also collected by aircraft. In the United States, special aircraft fly into hurricanes to monitor what is happening.

Balloons filled with helium gas are sent into the atmosphere, carrying instruments that measure air pressure, temperature and humidity.

How strong are hurricanes?

Hurricanes are measured by their strength and by the damage they cause. There are five levels of hurricane, Category Five being the strongest. The wind speed of a Category One hurricane is 74 to 95 miles (119 to 153 kilometers) per hour. Category Five hurricanes reach speeds of more than 155 miles (249 kilometers) per hour.

How do satellites help?

Two types of weather satellites hover 22,000 miles (36,000 kilometers) above Earth's surface gathering data that helps meteorologists analyze storm clouds and keep a close watch on hurricanes.

Polar-orbiting satellites travel from North pole to South pole, collecting information about temperatures and photographing the entire surface of Earth, one section at a time.

Polar-orbiting satellite

Geostationary satellite

Geostationary satellites always stay above the same point on Earth's surface, photographing the changing cloud patterns below.

What on Earth?

How are hurricanes named?

Hurricanes are given male and female names alternately, and alphabetically. So, for example, **B**ob might be followed by **C**arol.

What Makes the Wind Blow?

Warm air rises and as it does, cold air rushes in to take its place. This movement of cold air is wind. The more warm air that rises—the more wind there will be to replace it. A hurricane is wind in one of its most **extreme** forms.

Why do hurricanes happen?

Hurricanes begin over tropical oceans close to the equator, the hottest part of the world. Wind builds up across the oceans there, picking up **moisture** (water vapor) as it goes. As warm, moist air rises, it forms clouds and thunderstorms. Earth's rotation (or spin) causes these storm winds to spiral into a hurricane.

When do hurricanes happen?

The hurricane season usually begins in June and ends in November. These are the **hottest** months in the tropics. Most hurricanes happen then, but some can happen earlier or later in the year. Climate changes may be affecting this pattern.

Satellite image of storm clouds
gathering over North America

What on Earth?

Which direction?

This hurricane over North
America will spin
counter-clockwise because
the wind flowing into it is
pulling it to the right. This is
called the Coriolis force.
South of the equator the
Coriolis force has the
opposite effect, pulling
winds to the left.

Why Are Hurricanes Seasonal?

It takes warm water and moist air to create a hurricane. Warm air picks up more moisture from the sea than cold air. So in summer a greater amount of warm, moist air rises from the oceans than at any other time of the year. Gusts of cold air (or wind) quickly sweep in. Hurricane winds that form in the middle of an ocean are much stronger than normal land winds.

What is a tornado?

When a hurricane reaches land, a tornado can form inside it. A tornado is a twisting column of spinning air that reaches down from a storm cloud to the ground. It can suck up anything in its path and bring hailstorms and torrential rain too.

How fast is the wind speed of a hurricane?

Land

Ice

Land

Land

Scientists use satellite images (*left*) to find out how fast winds are blowing. Hurricanes are shown in orange. When a tropical storm's winds hit 74 miles (119 kilometers) per hour it officially becomes a hurricane.

How long do hurricanes last?

A hurricane's path can cover a long distance and may take days to reach land. Even then a hurricane can keep going, and most last several days.

What on Earth?

Fast, faster, fastest!

The fastest recorded wind speed in a hurricane was 318 miles (512 kilometers) per hour. It hit New York, New England and Canada in 1938.

Do Hurricanes Slow Down?

Hurricanes need the warm, moist air over an ocean. The wind speed of a hurricane increases as it approaches land. When the hurricane hits land, it dies out because it gradually runs out of moisture.

Can hurricanes get stronger?

When a hurricane hits the Caribbean Islands, it picks up more moisture from the sea between each island. This makes it even stronger by the time it reaches the coast of the United States.

What on Earth?

Not all bad?

Hurricanes move hot air away from the tropics. They help balance heat and moisture around Earth. Without them large areas of the world would be too hot for animal or human life.

God of storms?

The word hurricane comes from the Spanish word *huracan*, which probably came from the name of the Mayan storm god, "Hunraken".

What Is a Storm Surge?

A storm surge is a huge wave of seawater that can engulf the coast when a hurricane hits land. Hurricanes create **sudden** changes in air pressure which can cause sea levels to rise and waves to crash inland in a mighty storm surge. A storm surge is usually the most dangerous part of a hurricane.

Where do storm surges happen?

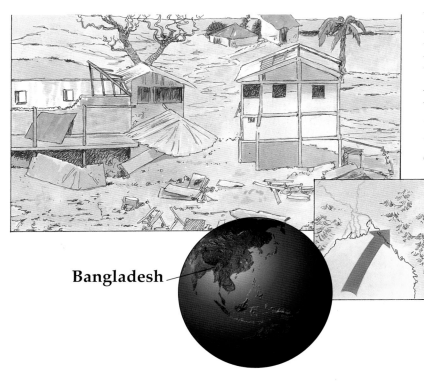

Bangladesh

Bangladesh, a country between Myanmar and India, is one of the places most affected by storm surges. It is very low-lying and has wide river estuaries. Huge storm surges travel far inland causing great destruction, especially when there is a high tide. In 1970 around 500,000 people died when a tropical cyclone hit this area.

The map (*left*) shows the direction from which storm surges hit Bangladesh.

How high?

The highest storm surge ever recorded was in Bathurst Bay, Australia, in 1899. The sea level rose by 43 feet (13 meters).

ow much damage can a storm surge cause?

In August 2005, Hurricane Katrina caused a storm surge which affected a coastline 1,264 miles (2,034 km) long. The huge flow of water led to floods up to 25 feet (7 meters) deep in the city of New Orleans, Louisiana, USA, and many towns were completely destroyed across three states.

19

What's the Damage?

Hurricanes are tremendously destructive, killing and injuring many people, and destroying homes and buildings. Crops are destroyed and power and water supplies, roads, bridges and railroad lines are **torn apart**. There can be widespread flood damage too.

What's the cost?

The cost of cleaning up and starting over after a hurricane is extremely high. It can take years to assess the total damage and add up the costs caused by a hurricane.

Boats swept inland by a storm surge add to the chaos after a storm.

What on Earth?

Which hurricane caused the most damage?

Hurricane Katrina in 2005 is thought to be the most expensive hurricane ever—costing even more than the 25 billion dollars worth of damage caused by Hurricane Andrew in 1992.

How Does Wildlife Cope?

Many animals sense that a storm is coming and head inland for safety. But the natural cycle of life for many birds, animals and insects is disrupted by a hurricane. Many animals die because their habitat is destroyed and their food source is wiped out.

How do creatures survive?

Some tropical bird species make round nests that are less likely to be blown around by the wind. Other species build nests close to the ground.

What on Earth?

Freedom!

Hurricane Andrew struck the Miami Metrozoo in the U.S.A. in August 1992, releasing monkeys and other wild animals from their pens.

Trees uprooted by a
hurricane can be replaced
by planting young trees.
However it will take a
very long time for them to
grow as big.

Are Hurricanes Getting Worse?

A re hurricanes getting fiercer and more frequent or can scientists just detect and monitor them better now? The world is having more extreme weather. Hurricanes, tornadoes and droughts are happening more often. Scientists think this extreme weather is caused by global warming.

What is global warming?

Scientists know that Earth is getting warmer. Some scientists argue that it is happening naturally. Other scientists feel that many things humans do are bad for Earth's climate. Worldwide use of fossil fuels such as coal and oil make a gas called carbon dioxide. This, and other gases, is heating up Earth. Is global warming making the weather more extreme? Some scientists say yes; some are not sure. Weather is still very unpredictable.

This satellite photograph (*right*) shows the path of Hurricane Andrew in 1992.

Desperation!

In 1998 during Hurricane Mitch, many parents in Honduras tied their children to the branches of tall trees to keep them from being swept away.

Can We Avoid Hurricanes?

A hurricane cannot be stopped, but with enough warning people can get out of its path. Countries that are most affected have 24-hour **warning** systems that provide frequent updates until the hurricane hits land. Meteorologists at national weather centers are linked to national radio and television networks and can provide warnings on the internet. Forecasting is not easy though, because a hurricane's path and wind-speed can quickly change making them unpredictable.

Does anything else help?

New building regulations in countries like Jamaica and Australia work to make structures safer. In the Caribbean Islands, the government is trying to develop special, shorter varieties of crops that can survive hurricane-force winds.

How Would You Survive a Hurricane?

If you live in an area that tends to have hurricanes, listen to all radio and television weather reports and advice. Warnings are helpful, but only when people act wisely. If you are ordered to evacuate, leave as soon as possible. Follow these simple steps to prepare for a hurricane.

Hurricane dangers

Storm surge Most people are killed by flooding during a hurricane. Follow hurricane warnings and evacuate as soon as possible.

Flying debris can kill. Doors, roofs and chimneys will be ripped from buildings, so avoid built-up areas.

Tornadoes Do not stay in your car because a powerful tornado can carry a car for as far as half a mile (one kilometer).

Travel will be hard, roads may be washed away and bridges destroyed.

What to do checklist

Be sure to wear **sturdy shoes,** you may have to travel far in difficult conditions. Make sure you have **cans of food** and a **can opener,** since the hurricane may last for days. Take all **pets** indoors. Board up windows with plywood so they won't break. A **generator** will supply you with electricity. Have a transistor **radio** and spare **batteries** so you can listen to updates on the hurricane. Have **money** because cash machines won't work and **water** because running water may stop. Cars should have a full tank of **gas** so you can travel after the storm.

Hurricane Facts

Huge hurricane waves called storm surges can reach up to 20 feet (7 meters) high! They destroy birds' nesting sites and kill thousands of fish.

Hurricane winds can rage for more than nine days across the ocean and on land.

The "eye" can be 20 miles (32 kilometers) wide from cloud wall to cloud wall!

In 1998, when Hurricane Georges hit islands in the Caribbean and the United States, twenty-eight tornadoes ran along with it.

In 2004, four hurricanes landed on the coast of Florida in just six weeks!

Hurricane Katrina, a Category Five storm, struck the Gulf coast of the United States on August 29th, 2005, causing massive devastation. Several towns and cities were evacuated and thousands of lives lost. It also caused the largest storm surge ever recorded on the east coast of America—up to 30 feet (9 meters) high.

Glossary

air pressure the force of air weighing down on a place

Coriolis force the effect that makes hurricanes spin in different directions depending on where they happen in the world

cyclone a hurricane in the southwest Pacific and Indian Oceans

equator imaginary line around Earth's widest part

habitat the natural home of a plant or animal

humidity warm, damp air

hurricane a vast spinning storm with winds over 74 miles (119 kilometers) per hour

Northern Hemisphere the top half of Earth

meteorologist a scientist who studies the weather

satellite a space technology system that orbits a planet recording information

tropics hot regions that lie north and south of the equator

typhoon a hurricane in the China Seas

water vapor an invisible gas made up of tiny droplets of water in the air

What Do You Know About Hurricanes?

1. What is a hurricane's "eye"?

2. Is there a hurricane season?

3. Is there any advance warning?

4. What is a cyclone?

5. Do hurricanes have names?

6. Why do hurricanes end?

7. What is a storm surge?

8. What creates a hurricane?

9. What was the most expensive hurricane?

10. Where do hurricanes form?

Can you guess what is different about this plane?

Go to page 32 for the answer!

Index

Pictures are shown in **bold.**

Answers

1. The calm area at the center of a hurricane (See page 5)
2. Yes! June to November (See page 12)
3. Yes. Sometimes animals sense a storm (See page 22)
5. Yes (See page 11)
6. They run out of moisture (See page 16)
7. A wall of seawater that crashes inland (See page 18)
8. Warm, moist air (See page 14)
9. To date, Hurricane Andrew in 1992, but the final cost of Katrina in 2005 is still unknown and is expected to be higher. (See page 21)
10. In warm tropical oceans around the equator (See page 8)

This plane can fly very **high**. It carries special equipment to measure and record the **strength** and direction of the wind.